DATE

This is a Dorling Kindersley Book
published by Random House, Inc.

Editors Andrea Pinnington,
Charlotte Davies
Designer Heather Blackham
Managing Editor Jane Yorke
Senior Art Editor Mark Richards
Photography Steve Gorton, Stephen Shott

Additional Photography Dave King
Models Amy Bradsell, Natalie Ellis,
Kiri Fisher, Kashi Gorton, Daniel Gregory,
Melanie Joannides, Paul Miller,
and Kimberley Yarde
Series Consultant Neil Morris

First American edition, 1991

Library of Congress Cataloging-in-Publication Data
My first look at clothes.
     p. cm.
     Originally published by Dorling Kindersley Ltd., London.
     Summary: Text and photographs depict what clothes are worn when it
is hot, when it is cold, when we go to bed, and when we go to the
seashore, and what clothes we put on first when getting dressed.
     ISBN 0-679-81806-5
     1. Clothing and dress – Juvenile literature. [1. Clothing and
dress.] I. Random House (Firm)
TT507.M9 1991
646'.36 - dc20
90-23999

Manufactured in Italy 1 2 3 4 5 6 7 8 9 10

Reproduced by Bright Arts, Hong Kong
Printed in Italy by L.E.G.O.

RST · LOOK · AT ·

Clothes

Random House New York

Getting dressed

Every morning I put on my clothes.

Today I am wearing purple overalls
and a yellow sweatshirt.

Underwear

When I get up, I put on my underwear.

socks

tights

undershirt

pants

Night clothes

I wear pajamas to bed.

nightie

pajamas

bàthrobe

slippers

Cold-day clothes

Brr! I need warm clothes on cold days.

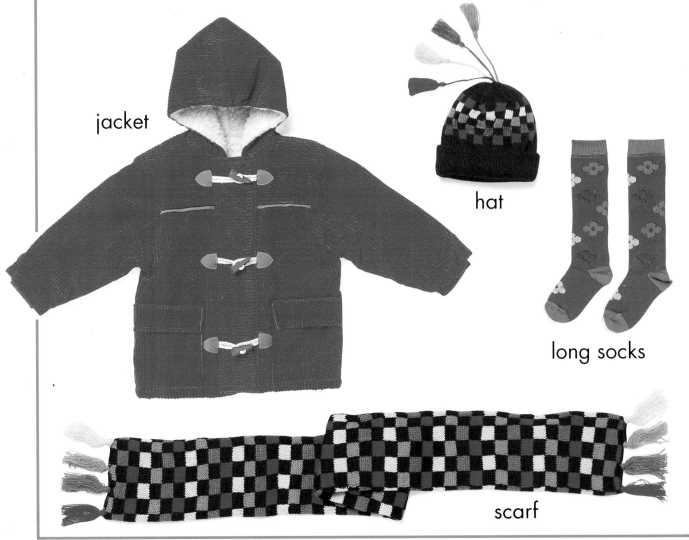

jacket

hat

long socks

scarf

gloves

mittens

sweater

pants

Hot-day clothes

When it's hot, I wear clothes that keep me cool.

sunglasses

skirt

T-shirt

shorts

swimsuit

sun hat

sundress

Dressing-up clothes

Who will we pretend to be?

pocketbook

straw hat

necklace

masks

feather boa

party hats

sword

scarf

belt

eye patch

pirate's hat

beard

Sportswear

I wear special clothes when I play sports.

kneepads

shorts

cap

sweat suit

sneakers

socks

flippers

goggles

headbands

football jersey

Shoes

Kids need so many kinds of shoes!

party shoes

boots

bootees

sandals

sneakers

oxfords

ballet shoes

Hat puzzle

Here are six different hats. Who would wear each of them?

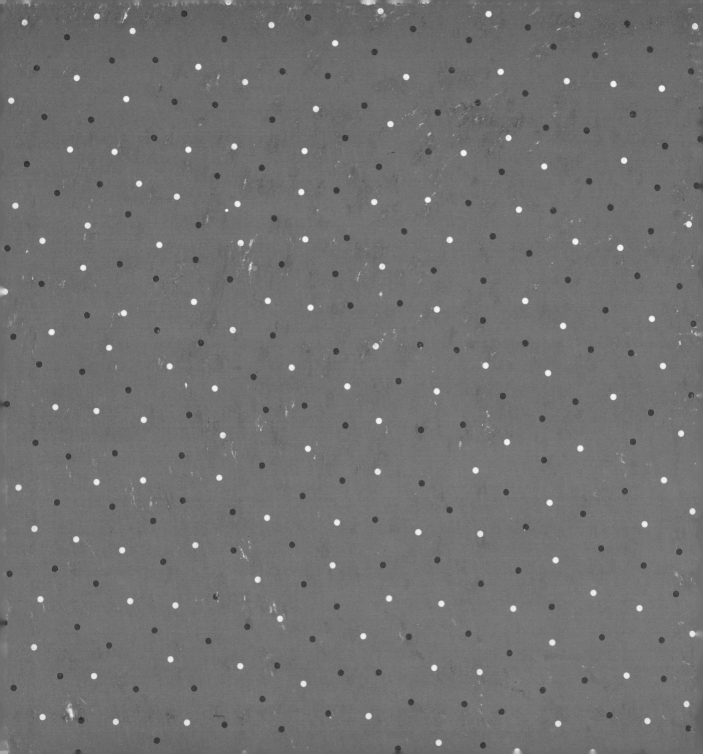